Tatian's Address to the Greeks

Tatian's Address to the Greeks

Tatian's Address to the Greeks

© Lighthouse Publishing 2018

All rights reserved. Without limiting the rights under copyright reserved above, no part of this publication may be reproduced, stored in a retrieval system, or transmitted, in any form or by any means (electronic, mechanical, photocopying, recording or otherwise), without the prior written permission of the copyright owner of this book.

Published by
Lighthouse Christian Publishing
SAN 257-4330
5531 Dufferin Drive
Savage, Minnesota, 55378
United States of America

www.lighthousechristianpublishing.com

Introductory Note
TO
Taitian the Assyrian

[[a.d. 110–172.] It was my first intention to make this author a mere appendix to his master, Justin Martyr; for he stands in an equivocal position, as half Father and half heretic. His good seems to have been largely due to Justin's teaching and influence. One may trust that his falling away, in the decline of life, is attributable to infirmity of mind and body; his severe asceticism countenancing this charitable thought. Many instances of human frailty, which the experience of ages has taught Christians to view with compassion rather than censure, are doubtless to be ascribed to mental aberration and decay. Early Christians had not yet been taught this lesson; for, socially, neither Judaism nor Paganism had wholly surrendered their unloving influences upon their minds. Moreover, their high valuation of discipline, as an essential condition of self-preservation amid the fires of surrounding scorn and hatred, led them to practice, perhaps too sternly, upon offenders, what they often heroically performed upon themselves,—the amputation of the scandalous hand, or the plucking out of the evil eye.

In Tatian, another Assyrian follows the Star of Bethlehem, from Euphrates and the Tigris. The scanty facts of his personal history are sufficiently detailed by the translator, in his Introductory Note. We owe to himself the pleasing story of his conversion from heathenism. But I think it important to qualify the impressions the translation may otherwise leave upon the student's mind, by a little more sympathy with the better side of his character, and a more just statement of his great services to the infant Church.

His works, which were very numerous, have perished, in consequence of his lapse from orthodoxy. Give him due credit for his *Diatessaron*, of which the very name is a valuable testimony to the Four Gospels as recognized by the primitive churches. It is lost, with the "infinite number" of other books which St. Jerome attributes to him. All honor to this earliest harmonist for such a work; and let us believe, with Mill and other learned authorities, that, if Eusebius had seen the work he censures, he might have expressed himself more charitably concerning it.

We know something of Tatian, already, from the melancholy pages of Irenæus. Theodoret finds no other fault with his *Diatessaron* than its omission of the genealogies, which he, probably, could not harmonize on any theory of his own. The errors into which he fell in his old age were so absurd, and so contrary to the Church's doctrine and discipline, that he could not be tolerated as one of the faithful, without giving to the heathen new grounds for the malignant slanders with which they were ever assailing the Christians. At the same time, let us reflect, that his fall is to be attributed to extravagant ideas of that encraty which is a precept of the Gospel, and which a pure abhorrence of pagan abominations led many of the orthodox to practice with extreme rigidity. And this is the place to say, once for all, that the figures of Elijah upon Mt. Carmel and of John Baptist in the wilderness, approved by our Lord's teachings, but moderated, as a lesson to others, by his own holy but less austere example, justify the early Church in making room for the two classes of Christians which must always be found in earnest religion, and which seem to have their warrant in the fundamental constitution of human nature. There must be men like St. Paul, living in the world, though not of it; and there must be men like the Baptist, of whom the world will say, "he hath a devil." Marvelously the early Catholics were piloted between the rocks and the whirlpools, in the narrow drift of the Gospel; and always the Holy Spirit of counsel and might was their guardian, amid their terrible trials and temptations. This must suggest, to every reflecting mind, a gratitude the most profound. To preserve evangelical encraty, and to restrain fanatical asceticism, was the spirit of early Christianity, as one sees in the ethics of Hermas. But the awful malaria of Montanism was even now rising like a fog of the marshes, and was destined to leave its lasting impress upon Western Christianity; "forbidding to marry, and commanding to abstain from meats." Our author, alas, laid the egg which Tertullian hatched, and invented terms which that great author raised to their highest power; for he was rather the disciple of Tatian than of the Phrygians, though they kindled his strange fire. After Tertullian, the whole subject of marriage became entangled with sophistries, which have ever since adhered to the Latin churches, and introduced the most corrosive results into the vitals of individuals and of nations. Southey suggests, that, in the Roman Communion, John Wesley would have been accommodated with full scope for his genius, and canonized as a saint, while his Anglican mother had no place for him. But, on the other hand, let us reflect that while Rome had no place for Wiclif and Hus, or Jerome of Prague, she has used and glorified and canonized many fanatics whose errors were far more disgraceful than those of Tatian and Tertullian. In fact, she would have utilized and beatified these very enthusiasts, had they risen in the Middle Ages, to combine their follies with equal extravagance in persecuting the Albigenses, while aggrandizing the papal ascendency.

I have enlarged upon the equivocal character of Tatian with melancholy interest, because I shall make sparing use of notes, in editing his sole surviving work, pronounced by Eusebius his masterpiece. I read it with sympathy, admiration, and instruction. I enjoy his biting satire of heathenism, his Pauline contempt for all philosophy save that of the Gospel, his touching reference to his own experiences, and his brilliant delineation of Christian innocence and of his own emancipation from the seductions of a deceitful and transient world. In short, I feel that Tatian deserves critical editing, in the original, at the hand and heart of some expert who can thoroughly appreciate his merits, and his relations to primitive Christianity.

The following is the original Introductory Notice:—

We learn from several sources that Tatian was an Assyrian, but know nothing very definite either as to the time or place of his birth. Epiphanius (*Hær.*, xlvi.) declares that he was a native of Mesopotamia; and we infer from other ascertained facts regarding him, that he flourished about the middle of the second century. He was at first an eager student of heathen literature, and seems to have been especially devoted to researches in philosophy. But he found no satisfaction in the bewildering mazes of Greek speculation, while he became utterly disgusted with what heathenism presented to him under the name of religion. In these circumstances, he happily met with the sacred books of the Christians, and was powerfully attracted by the purity of morals which these inculcated, and by the means of deliverance from the bondage of sin which they revealed. He seems to have embraced Christianity at Rome, where he became acquainted with Justin Martyr, and enjoyed the instructions of that eminent teacher of the Gospel. After the death of Justin, Tatian unfortunately fell under the influence of the Gnostic heresy, and founded an ascetic sect, which, from the rigid principles it professed, was called that of the Encratites, that is, "*The selfcontrolled*," or, "*The masters of themselves.*" Tatian latterly established himself at Antioch, and acquired a considerable number of disciples, who continued after his death to be distinguished by the practice of those austerities which he had enjoined. The sect of the Encratites is supposed to have been established about a.d. 166, and Tatian appears to have died some few years afterwards.

The only extant work of Tatian is his "Address to the Greeks." It is a most unsparing and direct exposure of the enormities of heathenism. Several other works are said to have been composed by Tatian; and of these, a *Diatessaron*, or *Harmony of the Four Gospels*, is specially mentioned. His Gnostic views led him to exclude from the continuous narrative of our Lord's life, given in this work, all those passages which bear upon the incarnation and true humanity of Christ. Not withstanding this defect, we cannot but regret the loss of this earliest Gospel harmony; but the very title it bore is important, as showing that the Four Gospels, and these only, were deemed authoritative about the middle of the second century.

CHAPTER I.—THE GREEKS CLAIM, WITHOUT REASON, THE INVENTION OF THE ARTS.

Be not, O Greeks, so very hostilely disposed towards the Barbarians, nor look with ill will on their opinions. For which of your institutions has not been derived from the Barbarians? The most eminent of the Telmessians invented the art of divining by dreams; the Carians, that of prognosticating by the stars; the Phrygians and the most ancient Isaurians, augury by the flight of birds; the Cyprians, the art of inspecting victims. To the Babylonians you owe astronomy; to the Persians, magic; to the Egyptians, geometry; to the Phoenicians, instruction by alphabetic writing. Cease, then, to miscall these imitations inventions of your own. Orpheus, again, taught you poetry and song; from him, too, you learned the mysteries. The Tuscans taught you the plastic art; from the annals of the Egyptians you learned to write history; you acquired the art of playing the flute from Marsyas and Olympus,—these two rustic Phrygians constructed the harmony of the shepherd's pipe. The Tyrrhenians invented the trumpet; the Cyclopes, the smith's art; and a woman who was formerly a queen of the Persians, as Hellanicus tells us, the method of joining together epistolary tablets: her name was Atossa. Wherefore lay aside this conceit, and be not ever boasting of your elegance of diction; for, while you applaud yourselves, your own people will of course side with you.

But it becomes a man of sense to wait for the testimony of others, and it becomes men to be of one accord also in the pronunciation of their language. But, as matters stand, to you alone it has happened not to speak alike even in common intercourse; for the way of speaking among the Dorians is not the same as that of the inhabitants of Attica, nor do the Æolians speak like the Ionians. And, since such a discrepancy exists where it ought not to be, I am at a loss whom to call a Greek. And, what is strangest of all, you hold in honor expressions not of native growth, and by the intermixture of barbaric words have made your language a medley. On this account we have renounced your wisdom, though I was once a great proficient in it; for, as the comic poet says,—

These are gleaners' grapes and small talk,—
Twittering places of swallows, corrupters of art.

Yet those who eagerly pursue it shout lustily, and croak like so many ravens. You have, too, contrived the art of rhetoric to serve injustice and slander, selling the free power of your speech for hire, and often representing the same thing at one time as right, at another time as not good. The poetic art, again, you employ to describe battles, and the amours of the gods, and the corruption of the soul.

CHAPTER II.—THE VICES AND ERRORS OF THE PHILOSOPHERS.

What noble thing have you produced by your pursuit of philosophy? Who of your most eminent men has been free from vain boasting? Diogenes, who made such a parade of his independence with his tub, was seized with a bowel complaint through eating a raw polypus, and so lost his life by gluttony. Aristippus, walking about in a purple robe, led a profligate life, in accordance with his professed opinions. Plato, a philosopher, was sold by Dionysius for his gormandizing propensities. And Aristotle, who absurdly placed a limit to Providence and made happiness to consist in the things which give pleasure, quite contrary to his duty as a preceptor flattered Alexander, forgetful that he was but a youth; and he, showing how well he had learned the lessons of his master, because his friend would not worship him shut him up and carried him about like a bear or a leopard. He in fact obeyed strictly the precepts of his teacher in displaying manliness and courage by feasting, and transfixing with his spear his intimate and most beloved friend, and then, under a semblance of grief, weeping and starving himself, that he might not incur the hatred of his friends. I could laugh at those also who in the present day adhere to his tenets,—people who say that sublunary things are not under the care of Providence; and so, being nearer the earth than the moon, and below its orbit, they themselves look after what is thus left uncared for; and as for those who have neither beauty, nor wealth, nor bodily strength, nor high birth, they have no happiness, according to Aristotle. Let such men philosophize, for me!

CHAPTER III.—RIDICULE OF THE PHILOSOPHERS.

I cannot approve of Heraclitus, who, being self-taught and arrogant, said, "I have explored myself." Nor can I praise him for hiding his poem5 in the temple of Artemis, in order that it might be published afterwards as a mystery; and those who take an interest in such things say that Euripides the tragic poet came there and read it, and, gradually learning it by heart, carefully handed down to posterity this darkness of Heraclitus. Death, however, demonstrated the stupidity of this man; for, being attacked by dropsy, as he had studied the art of medicine as well as philosophy, he plastered himself with cow-dung, which, as it hardened, contracted the flesh of his whole body, so that he was pulled in pieces, and thus died. Then, one cannot listen to Zeno, who declares that at the conflagration the same man will rise again to perform the same actions as before; for instance, Anytus and Miletus to accuse, Busiris to murder his guests, and Hercules to repeat his labors; and in this doctrine of the conflagration he introduces more wicked than just persons—one Socrates and a Hercules, and a few more of the same class, but not many, for the bad will be found far more numerous than the good. And according to him the Deity will manifestly be the author of evil, dwelling in sewers and worms, and in the perpetrators of impiety. The eruptions of fire in Sicily, moreover, confute the empty boasting of Empedocles, in that, though he was no god, he falsely almost gave himself out for one. I laugh, too, at the old wife's talk of Pherecydes, and the doctrine inherited from him by Pythagoras, and that of Plato, an imitation of his, though some think otherwise. And who would give his approval to the cynogamy of Crates, and not rather, repudiating the wild and tumid speech of those who resemble him, turn to the investigation of what truly deserves attention? Wherefore be not led away by the solemn assemblies of philosophers who are no philosophers, who dogmatize one against the other, though each one vents but the crude fancies of the moment. They have, moreover, many collisions among themselves; each one hates the other; they indulge in conflicting opinions, and their arrogance makes them eager for the highest places. It would better become them, moreover, not to pay court to kings unbidden, nor to flatter men at the head of affairs, but to wait till the great ones come to them.

CHAPTER IV.—THE CHRISTIANS WORSHIP GOD ALONE.

For what reason, men of Greece, do you wish to bring the civil powers, as in a pugilistic encounter, into collision with us? And, if I am not disposed to comply with the usages of some of them, why am I to be abhorred as a vile miscreant?7 Does the sovereign order the payment of tribute, I am ready to render it. Does my master command me to act as a bondsman and to serve, I acknowledge the serfdom. Man is to be honored as a fellowman; God alone is to be feared,—He who is not visible to human eyes, nor comes within the compass of human art. Only when I am commanded to deny Him, will I not obey, but will rather die than show myself false and ungrateful. Our God did not begin to be in time: He alone is without beginning, and He Himself is the beginning of all things. God is a Spirit, not pervading matter, but the Maker of material spirits, and of the forms that are in matter; He is invisible, impalpable, being Himself the Father of both sensible and invisible things. Him we know from His creation, and apprehend His invisible power by His works. I refuse to adore that workmanship which He has made for our sakes. The sun and moon were made for us: how, then, can I adore my own servants? How can I speak of stocks and stones as gods? For the Spirit that pervades matter is inferior to the more divine spirit; and this, even when assimilated to the soul, is not to be honored equally with the perfect God. Nor even ought the ineffable God to be presented with gifts; for He who is in want of nothing is not to be misrepresented by us as though He were indigent. But I will set forth our views more distinctly.

CHAPTER V.—THE DOCTRINE OF THE CHRISTIANS AS TO THE CREATION OF THE WORLD.

God was in the beginning; but the beginning, we have been taught, is the power of the Logos. For the Lord of the universe, who is Himself the necessary ground (ὑπόστασις) of all being, inasmuch as no creature was yet in existence, was alone; but inasmuch as He was all power, Himself the necessary ground of things visible and invisible, with Him were all things; with Him, by Logos-power (διὰ λογικῆς δυνάμεως), the Logos Himself also, who was in Him, subsists. And by His simple will the Logos springs forth; and the Logos, not coming forth in vain, becomes the first-begotten work of the Father. Him (the Logos) we know to be the beginning of the world. But He came into being by participation, not by abscission; for what is cut off is separated from the original substance, but that which comes by participation, making its choice of function, does not render him deficient from whom it is taken. For just as from one torch many fires are lighted, but the light of the first torch is not lessened by the kindling of many torches, so the Logos, coming forth from the Logos-power of the Father, has not divested of the Logos-power Him who begat Him. I myself, for instance, talk, and you hear; yet, certainly, I who converse do not become destitute of speech (λόγος) by the transmission of speech, but by the utterance of my voice I endeavor to reduce to order the unarranged matter in your minds. And as the Logos, begotten in the beginning, begat in turn our world, having first created for Himself the necessary matter, so also I, in imitation of the Logos, being begotten again, and having become possessed of the truth, am trying to reduce to order the confused matter which is kindred with myself. For matter is not, like God, without beginning, nor, as having no beginning, is of equal power with God; it is begotten, and not produced by any other being, but brought into existence by the Framer of all things alone.

CHAPTER VI.—CHRISTIANS' BELIEF IN THE RESURRECTION.

And on this account we believe that there will be a resurrection of bodies after the consummation of all things; not, as the Stoics affirm, according to the return of certain cycles, the same things being produced and destroyed for no useful purpose, but a resurrection once for all, when our periods of existence are completed, and in consequence solely of the constitution of things under which men alone live, for the purpose of passing judgment upon them. Nor is sentence upon us passed by Minos or Rhadamanthus, before whose decease not a single soul, according to the mythic tales, was judged; but the Creator, God Himself, becomes the arbiter. And, although you regard us as mere triflers and babblers, it troubles us not, since we have faith in this doctrine. For just as, not existing before I was born, I knew not who I was, and only existed in the potentiality (ὑπόστασις) of fleshly matter, but being born, after a former state of nothingness, I have obtained through my birth a certainty of my existence; in the same way, having been born, and through death existing no longer, and seen no longer, I shall exist again, just as before I was not, but was afterwards born. Even though fire destroy all traces of my flesh, the world receives the vaporized matter; and though dispersed through rivers and seas, or torn in pieces by wild beasts, I am laid up in the storehouses of a wealthy Lord. And, although the poor and the godless know not what is stored up, yet God the Sovereign, when He pleases, will restore the substance that is visible to Him alone to its pristine condition.

CHAPTER VII.—CONCERNING THE FALL OF MAN.

For the heavenly Logos, a spirit emanating from the Father and a Logos from the Logos-power, in imitation of the Father who begat Him made man an image of immortality, so that, as incorruption is with God, in like manner, man, sharing in a part of God, might have the immortal principle also. The Logos, too, before the creation of men, was the Framer of angels. And each of these two orders of creatures was made free to act as it pleased, not having the nature of good, which again is with God alone, but is brought to perfection in men through their freedom of choice, in order that the bad man may be justly punished, having become depraved through his own fault, but the just man be deservedly praised for his virtuous deeds, since in the exercise of his free choice he refrained from transgressing the will of God. Such is the constitution of things in reference to angels and men. And the power of the Logos, having in itself a faculty to foresee future events, not as fated, but as taking place by the choice of free agents, foretold from time to time the issues of things to come; it also became a forbidder of wickedness by means of prohibitions, and the encomiast of those who remained good. And, when men attached themselves to one who was more subtle than the rest, having regard to his being the first-born, and declared him to be God, though he was resisting the law of God, then the power of the Logos excluded the beginner of the folly and his adherents from all fellowship with Himself. And so he who was made in the likeness of God, since the more powerful spirit is separated from him, becomes mortal; but that first-begotten one through his transgression and ignorance becomes a demon; and they who imitated him, that is his illusions, are become a host of demons, and through their freedom of choice have been given up to their own infatuation.

CHAPTER VIII.—THE DEMONS SIN AMONG MANKIND.

But men form the material (ὑπόθεσις) of their apostasy. For, having shown them a plan of the position of the stars, like dice-players, they introduced Fate, a flagrant injustice. For the judge and the judged are made so by Fate; the murderers and the murdered, the wealthy and the needy, are the offspring of the same Fate; and every nativity is regarded as a theatrical entertainment by those beings of whom Homer says,—

"Among the gods
Rose laughter irrepressible."

But must not those who are spectators of single combats and are partisans on one side or the other, and he who marries and is a pæderast and an adulterer, who laughs and is angry, who flees and is wounded, be regarded as mortals? For, by whatever actions they manifest to men their characters, by these they prompt their hearers to copy their example. And are not the demons themselves, with Zeus at their head, subjected to Fate, being overpowered by the same passions as men? And, besides, how are those beings to be worshipped among whom there exists such a great contrariety of opinions? For Rhea, whom the inhabitants of the Phrygian mountains call Cybele, enacted emasculation on account of Attis, of whom she was enamored; but Aphrodité is delighted with conjugal embraces. Artemis is a poisoner; Apollo heals diseases. And after the decapitation of the Gorgon, the beloved of Poseidon, whence sprang the horse Pegasus and Chrysaor, Athené and Asclepios divided between them the drops of blood; and, while he saved men's lives by means of them, she, by the same blood, became a homicide and the instigator of wars. From regard to her reputation, as it appears to me, the Athenians attributed to the earth the son born of her connection with Hephæstos, that Athené might not be thought to be deprived of her virility by Hephæstos, as Atalanta by Meleager. This limping manufacturer of buckles and earrings, as is likely, deceived the motherless child and orphan with these girlish ornaments. Poseidon frequents the seas; Ares delights in wars; Apollo is a player on the cithara; Dionysus is absolute sovereign of the Thebans; Kronos is a tyrannicide; Zeus has intercourse with his own daughter, who becomes pregnant by him. I may instance, too, Eleusis, and the mystic Dragon, and Orpheus, who says,—

"Close the gates against the profane!"

Aïdoneus carries off Koré, and his deeds have been made into mysteries; Demeter bewails her daughter, and some persons are deceived by the Athenians. In the precincts of the temple of the son of Leto is a spot called Omphalos; but Omphalos is the burial-place of Dionysus. You now I laud, O Daphne!—by conquering the incontinence of Apollo, you disproved his power of vaticination; for, not foreseeing what would occur to you, he derived no advantage from his art. Let the far-shooting god tell me how Zephyrus slew Hyacinthus. Zephyrus conquered him; and in accordance with the saying of the tragic poet,—

"A breeze is the most honorable chariot of the gods,"—

conquered by a slight breeze, Apollo lost his beloved.

CHAPTER IX.—THEY GIVE RISE TO SUPERSTITIONS.

Such are the demons; these are they who laid down the doctrine of Fate. Their fundamental principle was the placing of animals in the heavens. For the creeping things on the earth, and those that swim in the waters, and the quadrupeds on the mountains, with which they lived when expelled from heaven,—these they dignified with celestial honor, in order that they might themselves be thought to remain in heaven, and, by placing the constellations there, might make to appear rational the irrational course of life on earth. Thus the high-spirited and he who is crushed with toil, the temperate and the intemperate, the indigent and the wealthy, are what they are simply from the controllers of their nativity. For the delineation of the zodiacal circle is the work of gods. And, when the light of one of them pre-dominates, as they express it, it deprives all the rest of their honor; and he who now is conquered, at another time gains the predominance. And the seven planets are well pleased with them, as if they were amusing themselves with dice. But we are superior to Fate, and instead of wandering (πλανητῶν) demons, we have learned to know one Lord who wanders not; and, as we do not follow the guidance of Fate, we reject its lawgivers. Tell me, I adjure you, did Triptolemus sow wheat and prove a benefactor to the Athenians after their sorrow? And why was not Demeter, before she lost her daughter, a benefactress to men? The Dog of Erigone is shown in the heavens, and the Scorpion the helper of Artemis, and Chiron the Centaur, and the divided Argo, and the Bear of Callisto. Yet how, before these performed the aforesaid deeds, were the heavens unadorned? And to whom will it not appear ridiculous that the Deltotum should be placed among the stars, according to some, on account of Sicily, or, as others say, on account of the first letter in the name of Zeus (Διός)? For why are not Sardinia and Cyprus honored in heaven? And why have not the letters of the names of the brothers of Zeus, who shared the kingdom with him, been fixed there too? And how is it that Kronos, who was put in chains and ejected from his kingdom, is constituted a manager of Fate? How, too, can he give kingdoms who no longer reigns himself? Reject, then, these absurdities, and do not become transgressors by hating us unjustly.

CHAPTER X.—RIDICULE OF THE HEATHEN DIVINITIES.

There are legends of the metamorphosis of men: with you the gods also are metamorphosed. Rhea becomes a tree; Zeus a dragon, on account of Persephone; the sisters of Phaëthon are changed into poplars, and Leto into a bird of little value, on whose account what is now Delos was called Ortygia. A god, forsooth, becomes a swan, or takes the form of an eagle, and, making Ganymede his cupbearer, glories in a vile affection. How can I reverence gods who are eager for presents, and angry if they do not receive them? Let them have their Fate! I am not willing to adore wandering stars. What is that hair of Berenicé? Where were her stars before her death? And how was the dead Antinous fixed as a beautiful youth in the moon? Who carried him thither: unless perchance, as men, perjuring themselves for hire, are credited when they say in ridicule of the gods that kings have ascended into heaven, so someone, in like manner, has put this man also among the gods, and been recompensed with honor and reward? Why have you robbed God? Why do you dishonor His workmanship? You sacrifice a sheep, and you adore the same animal. The Bull is in the heavens, and you slaughter its image. The Kneeler crushes a noxious animal; and the eagle that

devours the man-maker Prometheus is honored. The swan is noble, forsooth, because it was an adulterer; and the Dioscuri, living on alternate days, the ravishers of the daughters of Leucippus, are also noble! Better still is Helen, who forsook the flaxen-haired Menelaus, and followed the turbaned and gold-adorned Paris. A just man also is Sophron, who transported this adulteress to the Elysian fields! But even the daughter of Tyndarus is not gifted with immortality, and Euripides has wisely represented this woman as put to death by Orestes.

CHAPTER XI.—THE SIN OF MEN DUE NOT TO FATE, BUT TO FREE-WILL.

How, then, shall I admit this nativity according to Fate, when I see such managers of Fate? I do not wish to be a king; I am not anxious to be rich; I decline military command; I detest fornication; I am not impelled by an insatiable love of gain to go to sea; I do not contend for chaplets; I am free from a mad thirst for fame; I despise death; I am superior to every kind of disease; grief does not consume my soul. Am I a slave, I endure servitude. Am I free, I do not make a vaunt of my good birth. I see that the same sun is for all, and one death for all, whether they live in pleasure or destitution. The rich man sows, and the poor man partakes of the same sowing. The wealthiest die, and beggars have the same limits to their life. The rich lack many things, and are glorious only through the estimation they are held in; but the poor man and he who has very moderate desires, seeking as he does only the things suited to his lot, more easily obtains his purpose. How is it that you are fated to be sleepless through avarice? Why are you fated to grasp at things often, and often to die? Die to the world, repudiating the madness that is in it. Live to God, and by apprehending Him lay aside your old nature. We were not created to die, but we die by our own fault. Our free-will has destroyed us; we who were free have become slaves; we have been sold through sin. Nothing evil has been created by God; we ourselves have manifested wickedness; but we, who have manifested it, are able again to reject it.

CHAPTER XII.—THE TWO KINDS OF SPIRITS.

We recognize two varieties of spirit, one of which is called the soul (ψυχή), but the other is greater than the soul, an image and likeness of God: both existed in the first men, that in one sense they might be material (ὑλικοί), and in another superior to matter. The case stands thus: we can see that the whole structure of the world, and the whole creation, has been produced from matter, and the matter itself brought into existence by God; so that on the one hand it may be regarded as rude and unformed before it was separated into parts, and on the other as arranged in beauty and order after the separation was made. Therefore in that separation the heavens were made of matter, and the stars that are in them; and the earth and all that is upon it has a similar constitution: so that there is a common origin of all things. But, while such is the case, there yet are certain differences in the things made of matter, so that one is more beautiful, and another is beautiful but surpassed by something better. For as the constitution of the body is under one management, and is engaged in doing that which is the cause of its having been made, yet though this is the case, there are certain differences of dignity in it, and the eye is one thing, and another the ear, and another the arrangement of the hair and the distribution of the intestines, and the compacting together of the marrow and the bones and the tendons; and though one part differs from another, there is yet all the harmony of a concert of music in their arrangement;—in like manner the world, according to the power of its Maker containing some things of superior splendor, but some unlike these, received by the will of the Creator a material spirit. And these things severally it is possible for him to perceive who does not conceitedly reject those most divine explanations which in the course of time have been consigned to writing, and make those who study them great lovers of God. Therefore the demons, as you call them, having received their structure from matter and obtained the spirit which inheres in it, became intemperate and greedy; some few, indeed, turning to what was purer, but others choosing what was inferior in matter, and conforming their manner of life to it. These beings, produced from matter, but very remote from right conduct, you, O Greeks, worship. For, being turned by their own folly to vain gloriousness, and shaking off the reins [of authority], they have been forward to become robbers of Deity; and the Lord of all has suffered them to besport themselves, till the world, coming to an end, be dissolved, and the Judge appear, and all those men who, while assailed by the demons, strive after the knowledge of the perfect God obtain as the result of their conflicts a more perfect testimony in the day of judgment. There is, then, a spirit in the stars, a spirit in angels, a spirit in plants and the waters, a spirit in men, a spirit in animals; but, though one and the same, it has differences in itself. And while we say these things not from mere hearsay, nor from probable conjectures and sophistical reasoning, but using words of a certain diviner speech, do you who are willing hasten to learn. And you who do not reject with contempt the Scythian Anacharsis, do not disdain to be taught by those who follow a barbaric code of laws. Give at least as favorable a reception to our tenets as you would to the prognostications of the Babylonians. Hearken to us when we speak, if only as you would to an oracular oak. And yet the things just referred to are the trickeries of frenzied demons, while the doctrines we inculcate are far beyond the apprehension of the world.

CHAPTER XIII.—THEORY OF THE SOUL'S IMMORTALITY.

The soul is not in itself immortal, O Greeks, but mortal. Yet it is possible for it not to die. If, indeed, it knows not the truth, it dies, and is dissolved with the body, but rises again at last at the end of the world with the body, receiving death by punishment in immortality. But, again, if it acquires the knowledge of God, it dies not, although for a time it be dissolved. In itself it is darkness, and there is nothing luminous in it. And this is the meaning of the saying, "The darkness comprehendeth not the light." For the soul does not preserve the spirit, but is preserved by it, and the light comprehends the darkness. The Logos, in truth, is the light of God, but the ignorant soul is darkness. On this account, if it continues solitary, it tends downward towards matter, and dies with the flesh; but, if it enters into union with the Divine Spirit, it is no longer helpless, but ascends to the regions whither the Spirit guides it: for the dwelling-place of the spirit is above, but the origin of the soul is from beneath. Now, in the beginning the spirit was a constant companion of the soul, but the spirit forsook it because it was not willing to follow. Yet, retaining as it were a spark of its power, though unable by reason of the separation to discern the perfect, while seeking for God it fashioned to itself in its wandering many gods, following the sophistries of the demons. But the Spirit of God is not with all, but, taking up its abode with those who live justly, and intimately combining with the soul, by prophecies it announced hidden things to other souls. And the souls that are obedient to wisdom have attracted to themselves the cognate spirit; but the disobedient, rejecting the minister of the suffering God, have shown themselves to be fighters against God, rather than His worshippers.

CHAPTER XIV.—THE DEMONS SHALL BE PUNISHED MORE SEVERELY THAN MEN.

And such are you also, O Greeks,—profuse in words, but with minds strangely warped; and you acknowledge the dominion of many rather than the rule of one, accustoming yourselves to follow demons as if they were mighty. For, as the inhuman robber is wont to overpower those like himself by daring; so the demons, going to great lengths in wickedness, have utterly deceived the souls among you which are left to themselves by ignorance and false appearances. These beings do not indeed die easily, for they do not partake of flesh; but while living they practice the ways of death, and die themselves as often as they teach their followers to sin. Therefore, what is now their chief distinction, that they do not die like men, they will retain when about to suffer punishment: they will not partake of everlasting life, so as to receive this instead of death in a blessed immortality. And as we, to whom it now easily happens to die, afterwards receive the immortal with enjoyment, or the painful with immortality, so the demons, who abuse the present life to purposes of wrongdoing, dying continually even while they live, will have hereafter the same immortality, like that which they had during the time they lived, but in its nature like that of men, who voluntarily performed what the demons prescribed to them during their lifetime. And do not fewer kinds of sin break out among men owing to the brevity of their lives, while on the part of these demons transgression is more abundant owing to their boundless existence?

CHAPTER XV.—NECESSITY OF A UNION WITH THE HOLY SPIRIT.

But further, it becomes us now to seek for what we once had, but have lost, to unite the soul with the Holy Spirit, and to strive after union with God. The human soul consists of many parts, and is not simple; it is composite, so as to manifest itself through the body; for neither could it ever appear by itself without the body, nor does the flesh rise again without the soul. Man is not, as the croaking philosophers say, merely a rational animal, capable of understanding and knowledge; for, according to them, even irrational creatures appear possessed of understanding and knowledge. But man alone is the image and likeness of God; and I mean by man, not one who performs actions similar to those of animals, but one who has advanced far beyond mere humanity—to God Himself. This question we have discussed more minutely in the treatise concerning animals. But the principal point to be spoken of now is, what is intended by the image and likeness of God. That which cannot be compared is no other than abstract being; but that which is compared is no other than that which is like. The perfect God is without flesh; but man is flesh. The bond of the flesh is the soul; that which encloses the soul is the flesh. Such is the nature of man's constitution; and, if it be like a temple, God is pleased to dwell in it by the spirit, His representative; but, if it be not such a habitation, man excels the wild beasts in articulate language only,—in other respects his manner of life is like theirs, as one who is not a likeness of God. But none of the demons possess flesh; their structure is spiritual, like that of fire or air. And only by those whom the Spirit of God dwells in and fortifies are the bodies of the demons easily seen, not at all by others,—I mean those who possess only soul; for the inferior has not the ability to apprehend the superior. On this account the nature of the demons has no place for repentance; for they are the reflection of matter and of wickedness. But matter desired to exercise lordship over the soul; and according to their free-will these gave laws of death to men; but men, after the loss of immortality, have conquered death by submitting to death in faith; and by repentance a call has been given to them, according to the word which says, "Since they were made a little lower than the angels." And, for everyone who has been conquered, it is possible again to conquer, if he rejects the condition which brings death. And what that is, may be easily seen by men who long for immortality.

CHAPTER XVI.—VAIN DISPLAY OF POWER BY THE DEMONS.

But the demons who rule over men are not the souls of men; for how should these be capable of action after death? unless man, who while living was void of understanding and power, should be believed when dead to be endowed with more of active power. But neither could this be the case, as we have shown elsewhere. And it is difficult to conceive that the immortal soul, which is impeded by the members of the body, should become more intelligent when it has migrated from it. For the demons, inspired with frenzy against men by reason of their own wickedness, pervert their minds, which already incline downwards, by various deceptive scenic representations, that they may be disabled from rising to the path that leads to heaven. But from us the things which are in the world are not hidden, and the divine is easily apprehended by us if the power that makes souls immortal visits us. The demons are seen also by the men possessed of soul, when, as sometimes, they exhibit themselves to men, either that they may be thought to be something, or as evil-disposed friends may do harm to them as to enemies, or afford occasions of doing them honor to those who resemble them. For, if it were possible, they would without doubt pull down heaven itself with the rest of creation. But now this they can by no means effect, for they have not the power; but they make war by means of the lower matter against the matter that is like themselves. Should any one wish to conquer them, let him repudiate matter. Being armed with the breastplate of the celestial Spirit, he will be able to preserve all that is encompassed by it. There are, indeed, diseases and disturbances of the matter that is in us; but, when such things happen, the demons ascribe the causes of them to themselves, and approach a man whenever disease lays hold of him. Sometimes they themselves disturb the habit of the body by a tempest of folly; but, being smitten by the word of God, they depart in terror, and the sick man is healed.

CHAPTER XVII.—THEY FALSELY PROMISE HEALTH TO THEIR VOTARIES.

Concerning the sympathies and antipathies of Democritus what can we say but this, that, according to the common saying, the man of Abdera is Abderiloquent? But, as he who gave the name to the city, a friend of Hercules as it is said, was devoured by the horses of Diomedes, so he who boasted of the Magian Ostanes will be delivered up in the day of consummation as fuel for the eternal fire. And you, if you do not cease from your laughter, will gain the same punishment as the jugglers. Wherefore, O Greeks, hearken to me, addressing you as from an eminence, nor in mockery transfer your own want of reason to the herald of the truth. A diseased affection (πάθος) is not destroyed by a counter-affection (ἀντιπάθεια), nor is a maniac cured by hanging little amulets of leather upon him. There are visitations of demons; and he who is sick, and he who says he is in love, and he who hates, and he who wishes to be revenged, accept them as helpers. And this is the method of their operation: just as the forms of alphabetic letters and the lines composed of them cannot of themselves indicate what is meant, but men have invented for themselves signs of their thoughts, knowing by their peculiar combination what the order of the letters was intended to express; so, in like manner, the various kinds of roots and the mutual relation of the sinews and bones can effect nothing of themselves, but are the elemental matter with which the depravity of the demons works, who have determined for what purpose each of them is available. And, when they see that men consent to be served by means of such things, they take them and make them their slaves. But how can it be honorable to minister to adulteries? How can it be noble to stimulate men in hating one another? Or how is it becoming to ascribe to matter the relief of the insane, and not to God? For by their art they turn men aside from the pious acknowledgment of God, leading them to place confidence in herbs and roots. But God, if He had prepared these things to effect just what men wish, would be a Producer of evil things; whereas He Himself produced everything which has good qualities, but the profligacy of the demons has made use of the productions of nature for evil purposes, and the appearance of evil which these wear is from them, and not from the perfect God. For how comes it to pass that when alive I was in no wise evil, but that now I am dead and can do nothing, my remains, which are incapable of motion or even sense, should effect something cognizable by the senses? And how shall he who has died by the most miserable death be able to assist in avenging any one? If this were possible, much more might he defend himself from his own enemy; being able to assist others, much more might he constitute himself his own avenger.

CHAPTER XVIII.—THEY DECEIVE, INSTEAD OF HEALING.

But medicine and everything included in it is an invention of the same kind. If anyone is healed by matter, through trusting to it, much more will he be healed by having recourse to the power of God. As noxious preparations are material compounds, so are curatives of the same nature. If, however, we reject the baser matter, some persons often endeavor to heal by a union of one of these bad things with some other, and will make use of the bad to attain the good. But, just as he who dines with a robber, though he may not be a robber himself, partakes of the punishment on account of his intimacy with him, so he who is not bad but associates with the bad, having dealings with them for some supposed good, will be punished by God the Judge for partnership in the same object. Why is he who trusts in the system of matter not willing to trust in God? For what reason do you not approach the more powerful Lord, but rather seek to cure yourself, like the dog with grass, or the stag with a viper, or the hog with river-crabs, or the lion with apes? Why you deify the objects of nature? And why, when you cure your neighbor, are you called a benefactor? Yield to the power of the Logos! The demons do not cure, but by their art make men their captives.

And the most admirable Justin58 has rightly denounced them as robbers. For, as it is the practice of some to capture persons and then to restore them to their friends for a ransom, so those who are esteemed gods, invading the bodies of certain persons, and producing a sense of their presence by dreams, command them to come forth into public, and in the sight of all, when they have taken their fill of the things of this world, fly away from the sick, and, destroying the disease which they had produced, restore men to their former state.

CHAPTER XIX.—DEPRAVITY LIES AT THE BOTTOM OF DEMON-WORSHIP.

But do you, who have not the perception of these things, be instructed by us who know them: though you do profess to despise death, and to be sufficient of yourselves for everything. But this is a discipline in which your philosophers are so greatly deficient, that some of them receive from the king of the Romans 600 aurei yearly, for no useful service they perform, but that they may not even wear a long beard without being paid for it! Crescens, who made his nest in the great city, surpassed all men in unnatural love (παιδεραστία), and was strongly addicted to the love of money. Yet this man, who professed to despise death, was so afraid of death, that he endeavored to inflict on Justin, and indeed on me, the punishment of death, as being an evil, because by proclaiming the truth he convicted the philosophers of being gluttons and cheats. But whom of the philosophers, save you only, was he accustomed to inveigh against? If you say, in agreement with

our tenets, that death is not to be dreaded, do not court death from an insane love of fame among men, like Anaxagoras, but become despisers of death by reason of the knowledge of God. The construction of the world is excellent, but the life men live in it is bad; and we may see those greeted with applause as in a solemn assembly who know not God. For what is divination? and why are ye deceived by it? It is a minister to thee of worldly lusts. You wish to make war, and you take Apollo as a counselor of slaughter. You want to carry off a maiden by force, and you select a divinity to be your accomplice. You are ill by your own fault; and, as Agamemnon wished for ten councilors, so you wish to have gods with you. Some woman by drinking water gets into a frenzy, and loses her senses by the fumes of frankincense, and you say that she has the gift of prophecy. Apollo was a prognosticator and a teacher of
soothsayers: in the matter of Daphne he deceived himself. An oak, forsooth, is oracular, and birds utter presages! And so you are inferior to animals and plants! It would surely be a fine thing for you to become a divining rod, or to assume the wings of a bird! He who makes you fond of money also foretells your getting rich; he who excites to seditions and wars also predicts victory in war. If you are superior to the passions, you will despise all worldly things. Do not abhor us who have made this attainment, but, repudiating the demons, follow the one God. "All things61 were made by Him, and without Him not one thing was made." If there is poison in natural productions, this has supervened through our sinfulness. I am able to show the perfect truth of these things; only do you hearken, and he who believes will understand.

CHAPTER XX.—THANKS ARE EVER DUE TO GOD.

Even if you be healed by drugs (I grant you that point by courtesy), yet it behoves you to give testimony of the cure to God. For the world still draws us down, and through weakness

I incline towards matter. For the wings of the soul were the perfect spirit, but, having cast this off through sin, it flutters like a nestling and falls to the ground. Having left the heavenly companionship, it hankers after communion with inferior things. The demons were driven forth to another abode; the first created human beings were expelled from their place: the one, indeed, were cast down from heaven; but the other were driven from earth, yet not out of this earth, but from a more excellent order of things than exists here now. And now it behoves us, yearning after that pristine state, to put aside everything that proves a hindrance. The heavens are not infinite, O man, but finite and bounded; and beyond them are the superior worlds which have not a change of seasons, by which various diseases are produced, but, partaking of every happy temperature, have perpetual day, and light unapproachable by men below. Those who have composed elaborate descriptions of the earth have given an account of its various regions so far as this was possible to man; but, being unable to speak of that which is beyond, because of the impossibility of personal observation, they have assigned as the cause the existence of tides; and that one sea is filled with weed, and another with mud; and that some localities are burnt up with heat, and others cold and frozen. We, however, have learned things which were unknown to us, through the teaching of the prophets, who, being fully persuaded that the heavenly spirit along with the soul will acquire a clothing of mortality, foretold things which other minds were unacquainted with. But it is possible for everyone who is naked to obtain this apparel, and to return to its ancient kindred.

CHAPTER XXI.—DOCTRINES OF THE CHRISTIANS AND GREEKS RESPECTING GOD COMPARED.

We do not act as fools, O Greeks, nor utter idle tales, when we announce that God was born in the form of a man. I call on you who reproach us to compare your mythical accounts with our narrations. Athené, as they say, took the form of Deïphobus for the sake of Hector, and the unshorn Phooebus for the sake of Admetus fed the trailing-footed oxen, and the spouse us came as an old woman to Semele. But, while you treat seriously such things, how can you deride us? Your Asclepios died, and he who ravished fifty virgins in one night at Thespiæ lost his life by delivering himself to the devouring flame. Prometheus, fastened to Caucasus, suffered punishment for his good deeds to men. According to you, Zeus is envious, and hides the dream65 from men, wishing their destruction. Wherefore, looking at your own memorials, vouchsafe us your approval, though it were only as dealing in legends similar to your own. We, however, do not deal in folly, but your legends are only idle tales. If you speak of the origin of the gods, you also declare them to be mortal. For what reason is Hera now never pregnant? Has she grown old? or is there no one to give you information? Believe me now, O Greeks, and do not resolve your myths and gods into allegory. If you attempt to do this, the divine nature as held by you is overthrown by your own selves; for, if the demons with you are such as they are said to be, they are worthless as to character; or, if regarded as symbols of the powers of nature, they are not what they are called. But I cannot be persuaded to pay religious homage to the natural elements, nor can I undertake to persuade my neighbour. And Metrodorus of Lampsacus, in his treatise concerning Homer, has argued very foolishly, turning everything into allegory. For he says that neither Hera, nor Athené, nor Zeus are what those persons suppose who consecrate to them sacred enclosures and groves, but parts of nature and certain arrangements of the elements. Hector also, and Achilles, and Agamemnon, and all the Greeks in general, and the Barbarians with Helen and Paris, being of the same nature, you will of course say are introduced merely for the sake of the machinery of the poem, not one of these personages having really existed. But these things we have put forth only for argument's sake; for it is not allowable even to compare our notion of God with those who are wallowing in matter and mud.

CHAPTER XXII.—RIDICULE OF THE SOLEMNITIES OF THE GREEKS.

And of what sort are your teachings? Who must not treat with contempt your solemn festivals, which, being held in honor of wicked demons, cover men with infamy? I have often seen a man[67]—and have been amazed to see, and the amazement has ended in contempt, to think how he is one thing internally, but outwardly counterfeits what he is not—giving himself excessive airs of daintiness and indulging in all sorts of effeminacy; sometimes darting his eyes about; sometimes throwing his hands hither and thither, and raving with his face smeared with mud; sometimes personating Aphrodité, sometimes Apollo; a solitary accuser of all the gods, an epitome of superstition, a vituperator of heroic deeds, an actor of murders, a chronicler of adultery, a storehouse of madness, a teacher of cynædi, an instigator of capital sentences;—and yet such a man is praised by all. But I have rejected all his falsehoods, his impiety, his practices,—in short, the man altogether. But you are led captive by such men, while you revile those who do not take a part in your pursuits. I have no mind to stand agape at a number of singers, nor do I desire to be affected in sympathy with a man when he is winking and gesticulating in an unnatural manner. What wonderful or extraordinary thing is performed among you? They utter ribaldry in affected tones, and go through indecent movements; your daughters and your sons behold them giving lessons in adultery on the stage. Admirable places, forsooth, are your lecture-rooms, where every base action perpetrated by night is proclaimed aloud, and the hearers are regaled with the utterance of infamous discourses! Admirable, too, are your mendacious poets, who by their fictions beguile their hearers from the truth!

CHAPTER XXIII.—OF THE PUGILISTS AND GLADIATORS.

I have seen men weighed down by bodily exercise, and carrying about the burden of their flesh, before whom rewards and chaplets are set, while the adjudicators cheer them on, not to deeds of virtue, but to rivalry in violence and discord; and he who excels in giving blows is crowned. These are the lesser evils; as for the greater, who would not shrink from telling them? Some, giving themselves up to idleness for the sake of profligacy, sell themselves to be killed; and the indigent barters himself away, while the rich man buys others to kill him. And for these the witnesses take their seats, and the boxers meet in single combat, for no reason whatever, nor does anyone come down into the arena to succor. Do such exhibitions as these redound to your credit? He who is chief among you collects a legion of bloodstained murderers, engaging to maintain them; and these ruffians are sent forth by him, and you assemble at the spectacle to be judges, partly of the wickedness of the adjudicator, and partly of that of the men who engage in the combat. And he who misses the murderous exhibition is grieved, because he was not doomed to be a spectator of wicked and impious and abominable deeds. You slaughter animals for the purpose of eating their flesh, and you purchase men to supply a cannibal banquet for the soul, nourishing it by the most impious blood shedding. The robber commits murder for the sake of plunder, but the rich man purchases gladiators for the sake of their being killed.

CHAPTER XXIV.—OF THE OTHER PUBLIC AMUSEMENTS.

What advantage should I gain from him who is brought on the stage by Euripides raving mad, and acting the matricide of Alcmæon; who does not even retain his natural behavior, but with his mouth wide open goes about sword in hand, and, screaming aloud, is burned to death, habited in a robe unfit for man? Away, too, with the mythical tales of Acusilaus, and Menander, a versifier of the same class! And why should I admire the mythic piper? Why should I busy myself about the Theban Antigenides, like Aristoxenus? We leave you to these worthless things; and do you either believe our doctrines, or, like us, give up yours.

CHAPTER XXV.—BOASTINGS AND QUARRELS OF THE PHILOSOPHERS.

What great and wonderful things have your philosophers effected? They leave uncovered one of their shoulders; they let their hair grow long; they cultivate their beards; their nails are like the claws of wild beasts. Though they say that they want nothing, yet, like Proteus, they need a currier for their wallet, and a weaver for their mantle, and a wood-cutter for their staff, and the rich, and a cook also for their gluttony. O man competing with the dog, you know not God, and so have turned to the imitation of an irrational animal. You cry out in public with an assumption of authority, and take upon you to avenge your own self; and if you receive nothing, you indulge in abuse, and philosophy is with you the art of getting money. You follow the doctrines of Plato, and a disciple of Epicurus lifts up his voice to oppose you. Again, you wish to be a disciple of Aristotle, and a follower of Democritus rails at you. Pythagoras says that he was Euphorbus, and he is the heir of the doctrine of Pherecydes; but Aristotle impugns the immortality of the soul. You who receive from your predecessors doctrines which clash with one another, you the inharmonious, are fighting against the harmonious. One of you asserts that God is body, but I assert that He is without body; that the world is indestructible, but I say that it is to be destroyed; that a conflagration will take place at various times, but I say that it will come to pass once for all; that Minos and Rhadamanthus are judges, but I say that God Himself is Judge; that the soul alone is endowed with immortality, but I say that the flesh also is endowed with it. What injury do we inflict upon you, O Greeks? Why do you hate those who follow the word of God, as if they were the vilest of mankind? It is not we who eat human flesh—they among you who assert such a thing have been suborned as false witnesses; it is among you that Pelops is made a supper for the gods, although beloved by Poseidon, and Kronos devours his children, and Zeus swallows Metis.

CHAPTER XXVI.—RIDICULE OF THE STUDIES OF THE GREEKS.

Cease to make a parade of sayings which you have derived from others, and to deck yourselves like the daw in borrowed plumes. If each state were to take away its contribution to your speech, your fallacies would lose their power. While inquiring what God is, you are ignorant of what is in yourselves; and, while staring all agape at the sky, you stumble into pitfalls. The reading of your books is like walking through a labyrinth, and their readers resemble the cask of the Danaïds. Why do you divide time, saying that one part is past, and another present, and another future? For how can the future be passing when the present exists? As those who are sailing imagine in their ignorance, as the ship is borne along, that the hills are in motion, so you do not know that it is you who are passing along, but that time (ὁ αἰών) remains present as long as the Creator wills it to exist. Why am I called to account for uttering my opinions, and why are you in such haste to put them all down? Were not you born in the same manner as ourselves, and placed under the same government of the world? Why say that wisdom is with you alone, who have not another sun, nor other risings of the stars, nor a more distinguished origin, nor a death preferable to that of other men? The grammarians have been the beginning of this idle talk; and you who parcel out wisdom are cut off from the wisdom that is according to truth, and assign the names of the several parts to particular men; and you know not God, but in your fierce contentions destroy one another. And on this account you are all nothing worth. While you arrogate to yourselves the sole right of discussion, you discourse like the blind man with the deaf. Why do you handle the builder's tools without knowing how to build? Why do you busy yourselves with words, while you keep aloof from deeds, puffed up with praise, but cast down by misfortunes? Your modes of acting are contrary to reason, for you make a pompons appearance in public, but hide your teaching in corners. Finding you to be such men as these, we have abandoned you, and no longer concern ourselves with your tenets, but follow the word of God. Why, O man, do you set the letters of the alphabet at war with one another? Why do you, as in a boxing match, make their sounds clash together with your mincing Attic way of speaking, whereas you ought to speak more according to nature? For if you adopt the Attic dialect though not an Athenian, pray why do you not speak like the Dorians? How is it that one appears to you more rugged, the other more pleasant for intercourse?

CHAPTER XXVII.—THE CHRISTIANS ARE HATED UNJUSTLY.

And if you adhere to *their* teaching, why do you fight against me for choosing such views of doctrine as I approve? Is it not unreasonable that, while the robber is not to be punished for the name he bears, but only when the truth about him has been clearly ascertained, yet we are to be assailed with abuse on a judgment formed without examination? Diagoras was an Athenian, but you punished him for divulging the Athenian mysteries; yet you who read his Phrygian discourses hate us. You possess the commentaries of Leo, and are displeased with our refutations of them; and having in your hands the opinions of Apion concerning the Egyptian gods, you denounce us as most impious. The tomb of Olympian Zeus is shown among you, though someone says that the Cretans are liars. Your assembly of many gods is nothing. Though their despiser Epicurus acts as a torch-bearer, I do not any the more conceal from the rulers that view of God which I hold in relation to His government of the universe. Why do you advise me to be false to my principles? Why do you who say that you despise death exhort us to use art in order to escape it? I have not the heart of a deer; but your zeal for dialectics resembles the loquacity of

Thersites. How can I believe one who tells me that the sun is a red-hot mass and the moon an earth? Such assertions are mere logomachies, and not a sober exposition of truth. How can it be otherwise than foolish to credit the books of Herodotus relating to the history of Hercules, which tell of an upper earth from which the lion came down that was killed by Hercules? And what avails the Attic style, the sorites of philosophers, the plausibilities of syllogisms, the measurements of the earth, the positions of the stars, and the course of the sun? To be occupied in such inquiries is the work of one who imposes opinions on himself as if they were laws.

CHAPTER XXVIII.—CONDEMNATION OF THE GREEK LEGISLATION.

On this account I reject your legislation also; for there ought to be one common polity for all; but now there are as many different codes as there are states, so that things held disgraceful in some are honorable in others. The Greeks consider intercourse with a mother as unlawful, but this practice is esteemed most becoming by the Persian Magi; pæderasty is condemned by the Barbarians, but by the Romans, who endeavor to collect herds of boys like grazing horses, it is honored with certain privileges.

CHAPTER XXIX.—ACCOUNT OF TATIAN'S CONVERSION.

Wherefore, having seen these things, and moreover also having been admitted to the mysteries, and having everywhere examined the religious rites performed by the effeminate and the pathic, and having found among the Romans their Latiarian Jupiter delighting in human gore and the blood of slaughtered men, and Artemis not far from the great city sanctioning acts of the same kind, and one demon here and another there instigating to the perpetration of evil,— retiring by myself, I sought how I might be able to discover the truth. And, while I was giving my most earnest attention to the matter, I happened to meet with certain barbaric writings, too old to be compared with the opinions of the Greeks, and too divine to be compared with their errors; and I was led to put faith in these by the unpretending cast of the language, the inartificial character of the writers, the foreknowledge displayed of future events, the excellent quality of the precepts, and the declaration of the government of the universe as centered in one Being. And, my soul being taught of God, I discern that the former class of writings lead to condemnation, but that these put an end to the slavery that is in the world, and rescue us from a multiplicity of rulers and ten thousand tyrants, while they give us, not indeed what we had not before received, but what we had received but were prevented by error from retaining.

CHAPTER XXX.—HOW HE RESOLVED TO RESIST THE DEVIL.

Therefore, being initiated and instructed in these things, I wish to put away my former errors as the follies of childhood. For we know that the nature of wickedness is like that of the smallest seeds; since it has waxed strong from a small beginning, but will again be destroyed if we obey the words of God and do not scatter ourselves. For He has become master of all we have by means of a certain "hidden treasure," which while we are digging for we are indeed covered with dust, but we secure it as our fixed possession. He who receives the whole of this treasure has obtained command of the most precious wealth. Let these things, then, be said to our friends. But to you Greeks what can I say, except to request you not to rail at those who are better than yourselves, nor if they are called Barbarians to make that an occasion of banter? For, if you are willing, you will be able to find out the cause of men's not being able to understand one another's language; for to those who wish to examine our principles I will give a simple and copious account of them.

CHAPTER XXXI.—THE PHILOSOPHY OF THE CHRISTIANS MORE ANCIENT THAN THAT OF THE GREEKS.

But now it seems proper for me to demonstrate that our philosophy is older than the systems of the Greeks. Moses and Homer shall be our limits, each of them being of great antiquity; the one being the oldest of poets and historians, and the other the founder of all barbarian wisdom. Let us, then, institute a comparison between them; and we shall find that our doctrines are older, not only than those of the Greeks, but than the invention of letters. And I will not bring forward witnesses from among ourselves, but rather have recourse to Greeks. To do the former would be foolish, because it would not be allowed by you; but the other will surprise you, when, by contending against you with your own weapons, I adduce arguments of which you had no suspicion. Now the poetry of Homer, his parentage, and the time in which he flourished have been investigated by the most ancient writers,—by Theagenes of Rhegium, who lived in the time of Cambyses, Stesimbrotus of Thasos and Antimachus of Colophon, Herodotus of Halicarnassus, and Dionysius the Olynthian; after them, by Ephorus of Cumæ, and Philochorus the Athenian, Megaclides and Chamæleon the Peripatetics; afterwards by the grammarians, Zenodotus, Aristophanes, Callimachus,
Crates, Eratosthenes, Aristarchus, and Apollodorus. Of these, Crates says that he flourished before the return of the Heraclidæ, and within 80 years after the Trojan war; Eratosthenes says that it was after the 100th year from the taking of Ilium; Aristarchus, that it was about the time of the Ionian migration, which was 140 years after that event; but, according to Philochorus, after the Ionian migration, in the archonship of Archippus at Athens, 180 years after the Trojan war; Apollodorus says it was 100 years after the Ionian migration, which would be 240 years after the Trojan war. Some say that he lived 90 years before the Olympiads, which would be 317 years after the taking of Troy. Others carry it down to a later date, and say that Homer was a contemporary

of Archilochus; but Archilochus flourished about the 23d Olympiad, in the time of Gyges the Lydian, 500 years after Troy. Thus, concerning the age of the aforesaid poet, I mean Homer, and the discrepancies of those who have spoken of him, we have said enough in a summary manner for those who are able to investigate with accuracy. For it is possible to show that the opinions held about the facts themselves also are false. For, where the assigned dates do not agree together, it is impossible that the history should be true. For what is the cause of error in writing, but the narrating of things that are not true?

CHAPTER XXXII.—THE DOCTRINE OF THE CHRISTIANS, IS OPPOSED TO DISSENSIONS, AND FITTED FOR ALL.

But with us there is no desire of vainglory, nor do we indulge in a variety of opinions. For having renounced the popular and earthly, and obeying the commands of God, and following the law of the Father of immortality, we reject everything which rests upon human opinion. Not only do the rich among us pursue our philosophy, but the poor enjoy instruction gratuitously; for the things which come from God surpass the requital of worldly gifts. Thus we admit all who desire to hear, even old women and striplings; and, in short, persons of every age are treated by us with respect, but every kind of licentiousness is kept at a distance. And in speaking we do not utter falsehood. It would be an excellent thing if your continuance in unbelief should receive a check; but, however that may be, let our cause remain confirmed by the judgment pronounced by God. Laugh, if you please; but you will have to weep hereafter. Is it not absurd that Nestor, who was slow at cutting his horses' reins owing to his weak and sluggish old age, is, according to you, to be admired for attempting to rival the young men in fighting, while you deride those among us who struggle against old age and occupy themselves with the things pertaining to God? Who would not laugh when you tell us that the Amazons, and Semiramis, and certain other warlike women existed, while you cast reproaches on our maidens?

Achilles was a youth, yet is believed to have been very magnanimous; and Neoptolemus was younger, but strong; Philoctetes was weak, but the divinity had need of him against Troy. What sort of man was Thersites? yet he held a command in the army, and, if he had not through doltishness had such an unbridled tongue, he would not have been reproached for being peak-headed and bald. As for those who wish to learn our philosophy, we do not test them by their looks, nor do we judge of those who come to us by their outward appearance; for we argue that there may be strength of mind in all, though they may be weak in body. But your proceedings are full of envy and abundant stupidity.

CHAPTER XXXIII.—VINDICATION OF CHRISTIAN WOMEN.

Therefore I have been desirous to prove from the things which are esteemed honorable among you, that our institutions are marked by sober-mindedness, but that yours are in close affinity with madness. You who say that we talk nonsense among women and boys, among maidens and old women, and scoff at us for not being with you, hear what silliness prevails among the Greeks. For their works of art are devoted to worthless objects, while they are held in higher estimation by you than even your gods; and you behave yourselves unbecomingly in what relates to woman. For Lysippus cast a statue of Praxilla, whose poems contain nothing useful, and Menestratus one of Learchis, and Selanion one of Sappho the courtezan, and Naucydes one of Erinna the Lesbian, and Boiscus one of Myrtis, and Cephisodotus one of Myro of Byzantium, and Gomphus one of Praxigoris, and Amphistratus one of Clito. And what shall I say about Anyta, Telesilla, and Mystis? Of the first Euthycrates and Cephisodotus made a statue, and of the second Niceratus, and of the third Aristodotus; Euthycrates made one of Mnesiarchis the Ephesian, Selanion one of Corinna, and Euthycrates one of Thalarchis the Argive. My object in referring to these women is, that you may not regard as something strange what you find among us, and that, comparing the statues which are before your eyes, you may not treat the women with scorn who among us pursue philosophy. This Sappho is a lewd, love-sick female, and sings her own wantonness; but all our women are chaste, and the maidens at their distaffs sing of divine things more nobly than that damsel of yours. Wherefore be ashamed, you who are professed disciples of women yet scoff at those of the sex who hold our doctrine, as well as at the solemn assemblies they frequent. What a noble infant did Glaucippé present to you, who brought forth a prodigy, as is shown by her statue cast by Niceratus, the son of Euctemon the Athenian! But, if Glaucippé brought forth an elephant, was that a reason why she should enjoy public honors? Praxiteles and Herodotus made for you Phryné the courtezan, and Euthycrates cast a brazen statue of Panteuchis, who was pregnant by a whoremonger; and Dinomenes, because Besantis queen of the Pæonians gave birth to a black infant, took pains to preserve her memory by his art. I condemn Pythagoras too, who made a figure of Europa on the bull; and you also, who honor the accuser of Zeus on account of his artistic skill. And I ridicule the skill of Myron, who made a heifer and upon it a Victory because by carrying off the daughter of Agenor it had borne away the prize for adultery and lewdness. The Olynthian Herodotus made statues of Glycera the courtezan and Argeia the harper. Bryaxis made a statue of Pasiphaë; and, by having a memorial of her lewdness, it seems to have been almost your desire that the women of the present time should be like her. A certain Melanippë was a wise woman, and for that reason Lysistratus made her statue. But, forsooth, you will not believe that among us there are wise women!

CHAPTER XXXIV.—RIDICULE OF THE STATUES ERECTED BY THE GREEKS.

Worthy of very great honor, certainly, was the tyrant Bhalaris, who devoured sucklings, and accordingly is exhibited by the workmanship of Polystratus the Ambraciot, even to this day, as a very wonderful man! The Agrigentines dreaded to look on that countenance of his, because of his cannibalism; but people of culture now make it their boast that they behold him in his statue! Is it not shameful that fratricide is honored by you who look on the statues of Polynices and Eteocles, and that you have not rather buried them with their maker Pythagoras? Destroy these memorials of iniquity! Why should I contemplate with admiration the figure of the woman who bore thirty children, merely for the sake of the artist Periclymenus? One ought to turn away with disgust from one who bore off the fruits of great incontinence, and whom the Romans compared to a sow, which also on a like account, they say, was deemed worthy of a mystic worship. Ares committed adultery with Aphrodité, and Andron made an image of their offspring Harmonia. Sophron, who committed to writing trifles and absurdities, was more celebrated for his skill in casting metals, of which specimens exist even now. And not only have his tales kept the fabulist Æsop in everlasting remembrance, but also the plastic art of Aristodemus has increased his celebrity. How is it then that you, who have so many poetesses whose productions are mere trash, and innumerable courtezans, and worthless men, are not ashamed to slander the reputation of our women? What care I to know that Euanthé gave birth to an infant in the Peripatus, or to gape with wonder at the art of Callistratus, or to fix my gaze on the Neæra of Calliades? For she was a courtezan. Laïs was a prostitute, and Turnus made her a monument of prostitution. Why are you not ashamed of the fornication of Hephæstion, even though Philo has represented him very artistically? And for what reason do you honor the hermaphrodite Ganymede by Leochares, as if you possessed something admirable? Praxiteles even made a statue of a woman with the stain of impurity upon it. It behoved you, repudiating everything of this kind, to seek what is truly worthy of attention, and not to turn with disgust from our mode of life while receiving with approval the shameful productions of Philænis and Elephantis.

CHAPTER XXXV.—TATIAN SPEAKS AS AN EYE-WITNESS.

The things which I have thus set before you I have not learned at second hand. I have visited many lands; I have followed rhetoric, like yourselves; I have fallen in with many arts and inventions; and finally, when sojourning in the city of the Romans, I inspected the multiplicity of statues brought thither by you: for I do not attempt, as is the custom with many, to strengthen my own views by the opinions of others, but I wish to give you a distinct account of what I myself have seen and felt. So, bidding farewell to the arrogance of Romans and the idle talk of Athenians, and all their ill-connected opinions, I embraced our barbaric philosophy. I began to show how this was more ancient than your institutions, but left my task unfinished, in order to discuss a matter which demanded more immediate attention; but now it is time I should attempt to speak concerning its doctrines. Be not offended with our teaching, nor undertake an elaborate reply filled with trifling and ribaldry, saying, "Tatian, aspiring to be above the Greeks, above the infinite number of philosophic inquirers, has struck out a new path, and embraced the doctrines of Barbarians." For what grievance is it, that men manifestly ignorant should be reasoned with by a man of like nature with themselves? Or how can it be irrational, according to your own sophist, to grow old always learning something?

CHAPTER XXXVI.—TESTIMONY OF THE CHALDEANS TO THE ANTIQUITY OF MOSES.

But let Homer be not later than the Trojan war; let it be granted that he was contemporary with it, or even that he was in the army of Agamemnon, and, if any so please, that he lived before the invention of letters. The Moses before mentioned will be shown to have been many years older than the taking of Troy, and far more ancient than the building of Troy, or than Tros and Dardanus. To demonstrate this I will call in as witnesses the Chaldeans, the Phoenicians and the Egyptians. And what more need I say? For it behoves one who professes to persuade his hearers to make his narrative of events very concise. Berosus, a Babylonian, a priest of their god Belus, born in the time of Alexander, composed for Antiochus, the third after him, the history of the Chaldeans in three books; and, narrating the acts of the kings, he mentions one of them, Nabuchodonosor by name, who made war against the Phoenicians and the Jews,—events which we know were announced by our prophets, and which happened much later than the age of Moses, seventy years before the Persian empire. But Berosus is a very trustworthy man, and of this Juba is a witness, who, writing concerning the Assyrians, says that he learned the history from Berosus: there are two books of his concerning the Assyrians.

CHAPTER XXXVII.—TESTIMONY OF THE PHOENICIANS.

After the Chaldeans, the testimony of the Phoenicians is as follows. There were among them three men, Theodotus, Hypsicrates, and Mochus; Chaitus translated their books into Greek, and also composed with exactness the lives of the philosophers. Now, in the histories of the aforesaid writers it is shown that the abduction of Europa happened under one of the kings, and an account is given of the coming of Menelaus into Phoenicia, and of the matters relating to Chiramus, who gave his daughter in marriage to Solomon the king of the Jews, and supplied wood of all kind of trees for the building of the temple. Menander of Pergamus composed a history concerning the same things. But the age of Chiramus is somewhere about the Trojan war; but Solomon, the contemporary of Chiramus, lived much later than the age of Moses.

CHAPTER XXXVIII.—THE EGYPTIANS PLACE MOSES IN THE REIGN OF INACHUS.

Of the Egyptians also there are accurate chronicles. Ptolemy, not the king, but a priest of Mendes, is the interpreter of their affairs. This writer, narrating the acts of the kings, says that the departure of the Jews from Egypt to the places whither they went occurred in the time of king Amosis, under the leadership of Moses. He thus speaks: "Amosis lived in the time of king Inachus." After him, Apion the grammarian, a man most highly esteemed, in the fourth book of his Ægyptiaca (there are five books of his), besides many other things, says that Amosis destroyed Avaris in the time of the Argive Inachus, as the Mendesian Ptolemy wrote in his annals. But the time from Inachus to the taking of Troy occupies twenty generations. The steps of the demonstration are the following:—

CHAPTER XXXIX.—CATALOGUE OF THE ARGIVE KINGS.

The kings of the Argives were these: Inachus, Phoroneus, Apis, Criasis, Triopas, Argeius, Phorbas, Crotopas, Sthenelaus, Danaus, Lynceus, Proetus, Abas, Acrisius, Perseus, Sthenelaus, Eurystheus, Atreus, Thyestes, and Agamemnon, in the eighteenth year of whose reign Troy was taken. And every intelligent person will most carefully observe that, according to the tradition of the Greeks, they possessed no historical composition; for Cadmus, who taught them letters, came into Boeotia many generations later. But after Inachus, under Phoroneus, a check was with difficulty given to their savage and nomadic life, and they entered upon a new order of things. Wherefore, if Moses is shown to be contemporary with Inachus, he is four hundred years older than the Trojan war. But this is demonstrated from the succession of the Attic, [and of the Macedonian, the Ptolemaic, and the Antiochian] kings. Hence, if the most illustrious deeds among the Greeks were recorded and made known after Inachus, it is manifest that this must have been after Moses. In the time of Phoroneus, who was after Inachus, Ogygus is mentioned among the Athenians, in whose time was the first deluge; and in the time of Phorbas was Actæus, from whom Attica was called Actæa; and in the time of Triopas were Prometheus, and Epimetheus, and Atlas, and Cecrops of double nature, and Io; in the time of Crotopas was the burning of Phaëthon and the flood of Deucalion; in the time of Sthenelus was the reign of Amphictyon and the coming of Danaus into Peloponnesus, and the founding of Dardania by Dardanus, and the return of Europa from Phoenicia to Crete; in the time of Lynceus was the abduction of Koré, and the founding of the temple in Eleusis, and the husbandry of Triptolemus, and the coming of Cadmus to Thebes, and the reign of Minos; in the time of Proetus was the war of Eumolpus against the Athenians; in the time of Acrisius was the coming over of Pelops from Phrygia, and the coming of Ion to Athens, and the second Cecrops, and the deeds of Perseus and Dionysus, and Musæus, the disciple of Orpheus; and in the reign of Agamemnon Troy was taken.

CHAPTER XL.—MOSES MORE ANCIENT AND CREDIBLE THAN THE HEATHEN HEROES.

Therefore, from what has been said it is evident that Moses was older than the ancient heroes, wars, and demons. And we ought rather to believe him, who stands before them in point of age, than the Greeks, who, without being aware of it, drew his doctrines [as] from a fountain. For many of the sophists among them, stimulated by curiosity, endeavored to adulterate whatever they learned from Moses, and from those who have philosophized like him, first that they might be considered as having something of their own, and secondly, that covering up by a certain rhetorical artifice whatever things they did not understand, they might misrepresent the truth as if it were a fable. But what the learned among the Greeks have said concerning our polity and the history of our laws, and how many and what kind of men have written of these things, will be shown in the treatise against those who have discoursed of divine things.

CHAPTER XLI.

But the matter of principal importance is to endeavor with all accuracy to make it clear that Moses is not only older than Homer, but than all the writers that were before him— older than Linus, Philammon, Thamyris, Amphion, Musæus, Orpheus, Demodocus, Phemius, Sibylla, Epimenides of Crete, who came to Sparta, Aristæus of Proconnesus, who wrote the Arimaspia, Asbolus the Centaur, Isatis, Drymon, Euclus the Cyprian, Horus the Samian, and Pronapis the Athenian. Now, Linus was the teacher of Hercules, but Hercules preceded the Trojan war by one generation; and this is manifest from his son Tlepolemus, who served in the army against Troy. And Orpheus lived at the same time as Hercules; moreover, it is said that all the works attributed to him were composed by Onomacritus the Athenian, who lived during the reign of the Pisistratids, about the fiftieth Olympiad. Musæus was a disciple of Orpheus. Amphion, since he preceded the siege of Troy by two generations, forbids our collecting further particulars about him for those who are desirous of information. Demodocus and Phemius lived at the very time of the Trojan war; for the one resided with the suitors, and the other with the Phoeacians. Thamyris and Philammon were not much earlier than these. Thus, concerning their several performances in each kind, and their times and the record of them, we have written very fully, and, as I think, with all exactness. But, that we may complete what is still wanting, I will give my explanation respecting the men who are esteemed wise. Minos, who has been thought to excel in every kind of wisdom, and mental acuteness, and legislative capacity, lived in the time of Lynceus, who reigned after Danaus in the eleventh generation after Inachus. Lycurgus, who was born long after the taking of Troy, gave laws to the Lacedemonians. Draco is found to have lived about the thirty-ninth Olympiad, Solon about the forty-sixth, and Pythagoras about the sixty-second. We have shown that the Olympiads commenced 407 years after the taking of Troy. These facts being demonstrated, we shall briefly remark concerning the age of the seven wise men. The oldest of these, Thales, lived about the fiftieth Olympiad; and I have already spoken briefly of those who came after him.

CHAPTER XLII.—CONCLUDING STATEMENT AS TO THE AUTHOR.

These things, O Greeks, I Tatian, a disciple of the barbarian philosophy, have composed for you. I was born in the land of the Assyrians, having been first instructed in your doctrines, and afterwards in those which I now undertake to proclaim. Henceforward, knowing who God is and what is His work, I present myself to you prepared for an examination concerning my doctrines, while I adhere immoveably to that mode of life which is according to God.

Fragments. *I.*

In his treatise, *Concerning Perfection according to the Savior*, he writes, "Consent indeed fits for prayer, but fellowship in corruption weakens supplication. At any rate, by the permission he certainly, though delicately, forbids; for while he permits them to return to the same on account of Satan and incontinence, he exhibits a man who will attempt to serve two masters—God by the 'consent' (1 Cor. 7:5), but by want of consent, incontinence, fornication, and the devil."— Clem. Alex.: *Strom.*, iii. c. 12.

II.

A certain person inveighs against generation, calling it corruptible and destructive; and someone does violence [to Scripture], applying to pro-creation the Savior's words, "Lay not up treasure on earth, where moth and rust corrupt;" and he is not ashamed to add to these the words of the prophet: "You all shall grow old as a garment, and the moth shall devour you." And, in like manner, they adduce the saying concerning the resurrection of the dead, "The sons of that world neither marry nor are given in marriage."—Clem. Alex.: iii. c. 12, § 86.

III.

Tatian, who maintaining the imaginary flesh of Christ, pronounces all sexual connection impure, who was also the very violent heresiarch of the Encratites, employs an argument of this sort: "If any one sows to the flesh, of the flesh he shall reap corruption;" but he sows to the flesh who is joined to a woman; therefore he who takes a wife and sows in the flesh, of the flesh he shall reap corruption.—Hieron.: *Com. in Ep. ad Gal.*

IV.

Seceding from the Church, and being elated and puffed up by a conceit of his teacher, as if he were superior to the rest, he formed his own peculiar type of doctrine. Imagining certain invisible Æons like those of Valentinus, and denouncing marriage as defilement and fornication in the same way as Marcion and Saturninus, and denying the salvation of Adam as an opinion of his own.—Irenæus: Adv. Hoer., i. 28.

V.

Tatian attempting from time to time to make use of Paul's language, that in Adam all die, but ignoring that "where sin abounded, grace has much more abounded."—Irenæus: *Adv. Heres.*, iii. 37.

VI.

Against Tatian, who says that the words, "Let there be light," are to be taken as a prayer. If He who uttered it knew a superior God, how is it that He says, "I am God, and there is none beside me"? He said that there are punishments for blasphemies, foolish talking, and licentious words, which are punished and chastised by the Logos. And he said that women were punished on account of their hair and ornaments by a power placed over those things, which also gave strength to Samson by his hair, and punishes those who by the ornament of their hair are urged on to fornication.—Clem. Alex.: *Frag.*

VII.

But Tatian, not understanding that the expression "Let there be" is not always precative but sometimes imperative, most impiously imagined concerning God, who said "Let there be light," that He prayed rather than commanded light to be, as if, as he impiously thought, God was in darkness.—Origen: *De Orat.*

VIII.

Tatian separates the old man and the new, but not, as we say, understanding the old man to be the law, and the new man to be the Gospel. We agree with him in saying the same thing, but not in the sense he wishes, abrogating the law as if it belonged to another God.—Clem. Alex.: *Strom.*, iii. 12.

IX.

Tatian condemns and rejects not only marriage, but also meats which God has created for use.—Hieron.: *Adv. Jovin.*, i. 3.

X.

"But ye gave the Nazarites wine to drink, and commanded the prophets, saying, Prophesy not." On this, perhaps, Tatian the chief of the Encratites endeavors to build his heresy, asserting that wine is not to be drunk, since it was commanded in the law that the Nazarites were not to drink wine, and now those who give the Nazarites wine are accused by the prophet.—Hieron.: *Com. in Amos.*

XI.

Tatian, the patriarch of the Encratites, who himself rejected some of Paul's Epistles, believed this especially, that is [addressed] to Titus, ought to be declared to be the apostle's, thinking little of the assertion of Marcion and others, who agree with him on this point.—Hieron.: *Præf. in Com. ad Tit.*

XII.

[Archelaus (a.d. 280), Bishop of Carrha in Mesopotamia, classes his countryman Tatian with "Marcion, Sabellius, and others who have made up for themselves a peculiar science," i.e., a theology of their own.—Routh: *Reliquiæ*, tom. v. p. 137. But see Edinburgh Series of this work, vol. xx. p. 267.]

www.ingramcontent.com/pod-product-compliance
Lightning Source LLC
Chambersburg PA
CBHW052043070526
44584CB00018B/2584